T0380957

To order additional copies of this book, contact:
Xlibris
1-800-455-039
www.xlibris.com.au
Orders@Xlibris.com.au

Peaceful Living

with Prayer and

Meditation

Joanne Jackett

Index of Prayers for 'Peaceful Living with Prayer and Meditation'

Prayers And Meditation At The Labyrinth

DEDICATION

For the Boys

Anthony, Michael and Tommy

With Love

and my Blessed Guru

Paramahunsa Yogananda

With Love and Thanks

To the Reader

Hello and Welcome to this collection of prayers and meditation.

Prayer and Meditation have been in my life for as long as I can remember. I think for that reason I am blessed to have experienced the profound effect that both prayer and meditation have had on my life.

We can pray for little every day things, for people or for hugely important challenges that we are called to face. We can also pray in thanksgiving and gratitude for blessings that come to us. Sincere prayer can help us through difficult times without dissolving into despair or crumbling in a heap. Even if there is despair or feelings of giving up, it is important that you try to realise these feelings will pass and instead, be kind and loving to yourself and perhaps pray even more deeply. All prayers are a way of reaching out to someone or something for help or gratitude. I would sincerely like to suggest though, that when praying, you try not to come from a place of fear or even worse, unworthiness.

When praying to our Heavenly Father or Divine Mother or both, trust and believe that you are building a relationship with the Divine. These are not two entities, but one loving God. Over time we come to understand that we are profoundly loved. Be patient and keep on keeping on.

When you are praying, also give yourself time to relax and to allow tension in the physical body to release. This practice along with nice easy breathing helps to open the heart to receive God's blessings and grace. When you pray with sincerity and trust you are in fact in relationship and communication with your God. It is said that the true nature of pray is to listen. So consider while saying these prayers that you are actually talking to God. Then in the stillness of meditation, listen.

Answers to prayers are not always as we expect, or come when we expect them. They can come in most unexpected forms. Through our sincerity and receptivity both in prayer and in meditation, our intuition is alive and awake to the Divine grace and guidance that is given.

If it is helpful you may like to follow these easy steps to develop a daily practice.

1. Sit quietly. Eyes lightly closed. Feet on the floor with back upright, supported if you like. No rigidity.

2. Select your prayer and follow the suggestions given in relation to the prayer. Make sure that you feel relaxed and settled and that you can spend a minute or two with breath awareness.

3. Read the prayer out loud or silently. Feel every word. Read it as many times as you feel necessary. I often find that repetition helps to deepen my connection to the prayer and imprints the intention more deeply in the mind.

4. Then sit in stillness. Allow the essence of the prayer to rest in your heart. When the mind becomes entangled with restless thoughts, come back to breath awareness and the words of your prayer. You may need to do this a number of times. Be peaceful, be relaxed. This is a fundamental technique for meditation practice.

5. When the time has come to complete your meditation, give thanks and resolve to practice again.

I wish you many blessings and many years ahead of Peaceful Living, with Prayer and Meditation.

Joanne.

A Prayer for our Planet Earth

Relax and be still as you feel this prayer coming from the heart. Say these words not with a sense of worry or anger or frustration but rather with a sense of trust and belief. Feel that the love for our planet earth and all sentient beings is placed in God's care and that we as human kind will respond to what is required of us to make our world and the planet a better place.

HEAVENLY FATHER

My prayer is for our planet earth.

I pray that all human kind become aware of the need to appreciate
what we have and not to keep wanting what we do not need.

I pray that we see the beauty in our world that is here for us, and
to know that this world, this precious world needs our love, care
and nurturing just like us as individual human beings.

Help us to open our eyes and see with compassion and love, what needs
to be done, and guide our reason will and action, always towards the
highest and the best for our planet and all sentient beings.

Thank you. Amen.

A short Morning Prayer

Upon waking, before thoughts of the day impact upon you, feel the evenness of breath and smile. This is an important prayer as it can set the tone, energy and mood for the day. Before you begin, tune in to the Heavenly Father as you ask for blessings and know that you are being heard and that you are loved. To do your best is all that God asks. Open your heart and feel the presence.

HEAVENLY FATHER

As I wake from sleep to live another day, please bless me.

I will fulfil all my responsibilities and show loving kindness
towards myself and those around me.

I do not know what you have planned for me so I will do
my best to hear your silent voice of guidance.

Protect me, bless me, be my guiding light.

Thank you. Amen

A Prayer with meditation
before the day begins

To pray in the morning, before your day begins is important. Know that it is laying a foundation of positivity and gratitude for the opportunity to experience another day. It also awakens awareness that we do not have to carry any burden of life on our shoulders all alone. It enlivens the law of attraction to work for you for the highest and best outcome. Begin with as much time as necessary to feel a gentle quietness descend upon you. Breathe evenly, then in the stillness feel this prayer coming from your heart that its essence will remain with you throughout the day.

Heavenly Father, Divine Mother

I begin the day with gratitude.

May that thought and feeling of gratitude continue in me throughout the day.

I know I am blessed to be here, to have this life which is so precious.

May I embrace every moment and live every moment fully.

May I be open and present to follow your guiding light.

May I realise that your light, is the light within me.

Bless this day for me and all sentient beings.

Thank you. Amen.

PRAYER FOR GUIDANCE

As the prayer suggests allow stillness to settle within you. Give yourself time to just be with the unfailing love and presence of God within. Be still, breathe evenly and naturally. Eyes lightly closed allowing your body to relax.

After you have said this prayer, sit quietly allowing peace to arise and feel fully receptive to God's Grace, Guidance and Love.

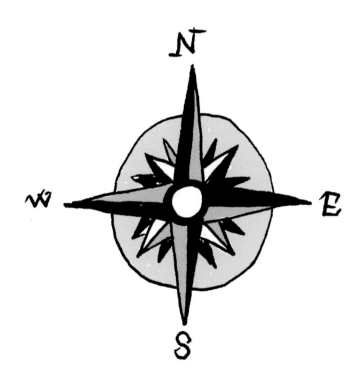

HEAVENLY FATHER

My stillness arises as I feel your loving presence within.

In this stillness, please allow me to hear your silent voice.

I ask for guidance and I can only hear and receive that
guidance in the stillness of my heart.

May I be receptive to your Divine will.

I shall reason, will and act according to your Divine will as I
know your plan for me is the highest and the best.

I hear and trust your silent voice.

Help me to release all that prevents me from hearing your precious words of guidance

May I rest in stillness and be guided in thought, word and action.

Thank you. Amen

A Prayer for Protection

As we travel through life there are many occasions when we are in need of protection, when we want to reach out for protection, when the mind is so restless, and we easily fall into the grip of negativity and doubt. In these moments, reach out to the Heavenly Father with sincerity and trust.

Pray with the desire to go beyond thoughts of negativity and to see a positive way ahead. After praying sit in stillness, using a calm breath rhythm to stay centred in your heart.

HEAVENLY FATHER

I ask for your protection. Please be with me through this journey of life.

With your guidance and my growing receptivity to that guidance, I will be safe.

In this body with this restless mind, I am subject to much negativity.

I know I am blessed with choice and free will to overcome all obstacles.

I pray that I always hear your loving words that guide me. That I feel them in my heart.

This is what strengthens me and holds my faith.

Protect me from the influence of negativity and may I see
clearly your divine plan and your unfailing love.

The love that gives me 'Wings of Power'*

Thank you. Amen.

*Wings of Power is the title of a book by my teacher Margrit Segesman

This Morning Prayer is addressed to Divine Mother, being the female aspect of our beloved God. This one can be said any time of course, but if you do your meditation practice in the morning, or you wish to commit to a morning meditation, this prayer may help you to feel settled and ready. So before you begin this prayer, be with calm relaxed breathing allowing any tension or tightness to leave the body. Be fully present, unhurried and sincere. Then having said the prayer once or as many times as you feel necessary, be conscious of your breathing as you move into a still quiet place within.

DIVINE MOTHER

Thank you, your love and light is with me this day as I move towards meditation.

As the day opens up and unfolds may I see you in everything and everyone.

May my heart be full of joy and feel your creative power present in all that I do.

I can relax and let go of all anxiety, fear and doubt, and know that all is well.

I know you are with me in every breath I take.

May stillness come to me now in meditation and also at times throughout
the day, to be the perfect reminder of your Divine presence in my life.

Bless me. Thank you. Amen

A Prayer when finding it difficult to pray

At times it can be difficult to find words that would address and express your deepest need. Just sit quietly, having removed yourself from distractions as much as you can. Try to let go of any limiting thoughts such as how much time you may have. Affirm to yourself that 'there is enough time'. Take a deep breath in and sigh the breath out. Repeat this three times. Then breathe evenly, feeling the natural rhythm of your body and breath. Allow yourself to relax as you breathe. It is likely that if your body is tense and you are feeling stressed that your mind and heart are unable to open to self nurturing and loving kindness. Say this prayer feeling the love of God is within and around you. Pray quietly with a genuine sense of patience and trust. Be open to where it takes you.

HEAVENLY FATHER

Help me to pray.

Teach me to pray. Teach me to listen.

May I find my inner silence and peace so that I feel your
Divine presence and hear your silent words.

May I sink deeply into the silence within myself where I may feel your presence and love.

I do not have to speak or ask for anything, as you know what is right for me.

Reveal Thyself within myself.

That is my prayer.

Thank you. Amen.

A Prayer for Creative Expression

To release creative power and direct it into whatever we wish to express, we must allow our restless, grasping mind to settle into a place of peace and calmness. Close your eyes and breathe with awareness until you are sure your breath is even and relaxed. Take your time and be patient. Please remember, there is enough time. You cannot rush. Calmness is the perfect environment for inspiration to flow.

Remember also to meditate daily or as often as you can with this prayer. Inspiration comes when you least expect it. Pray with sincerity, patience and trust.

HEAVENLY FATHER

I know that your creative power is within me and I ask that

you bless me now.

I know that I can trust you and I pray that my mind be
calm, so as to clearly receive your inspiration.

Help me to let go of resistance and allow your creative
power to flow into me and through me.

I believe in your guidance and the creative energy within me and the gifts
that you so generously grant according to your will and my receptivity.
With a peaceful mind, I rest in stillness. I am open and receptive to
receive your guidance and to hear your silent voice and inspiration.

Thank you. Amen

A Prayer for Clarity

To have a clear mind is to be receptive, and to be receptive one must be calm and relaxed. Sit quietly and feel the evenness of breath. Don't rush. Your prayer will be more effective when you are calm and sincere in how you pray.

DIVINE MOTHER

Clear my mind so all that I hear is your gentle voice of wisdom and love.

Without a clear mind I am entangled in negativity, doubt and restlessness. This does not serve my highest good.

I am only to feel your presence in my heart and I am no longer caught up in my restless mind.

As I breathe I feel quietness settling in my being.

As I breathe, I am in the presence of your divine love.

May clarity and peace come to me through your divine grace.

Be my beacon of light and may I grow in this faith.

Thank you. Amen.

A Prayer of Thanksgiving and Surrender

As you approach and pray to Divine Mother in this instance, feel a connection. Feel there is a mutual love and that sincerity and love shines from your heart and soul. This is a prayer that you might pray often, for the more we can feel gratitude and the more we can surrender to the Divine Plan, the more we are in a place of happiness and peace.

DIVINE MOTHER

I am praying from my heart that is filled with thankfulness and love.

Thank you for this precious life. I have obstacles to overcome I
know, but there are also many opportunities and blessings.

I know I can take refuge in you and realize your divine presence in me.

Guide my every move, my every thought.

May your divine grace heal me of all ignorance and protect me always.

Of my own self I can do nothing, (John 5.30) but with you all things are possible.

Divine Mother I am in your hands.

Help me to surrender fully for I know then that all is well.

Thank you. Amen

A Prayer for Anxiety

Take time to be still when you can. Even in the chaos and sometimes disturbance of life, find a quiet place. This quiet place may be found right within you, even while physically being in the centre of outer demands, expectations, feeling anxious and amidst the pressures of every day life. Train your mind to withdraw. Breathe calmly and patiently to meet the peace and stillness arising from the temple of quietness deep within yourself. Nothing can touch you in that still quiet place. Pray with sincerity and trust.

DIVINE MOTHER

As I pause in this quiet place, I become aware of your still presence in my heart.

As I breathe, I feel gratitude, safety and peace. I know that you are there.

Anxiety, fear and tension dissolve into my peaceful breathing.

I tune out all negative feelings and tune into your love and peace.

As this day unfolds may I hold your light and love and peace in my heart
and may I see these qualities also in the hearts of all sentient beings.

Thank you. Amen.

Physical pain can touch anyone at anytime. When saying this prayer try to relax and let go of any fear that may have arisen along with the pain. Breathe calmly and concentrate on the out breath relaxing your body more and more. With practice it is possible to allow the mind to be clear enough and receptive enough to ask for healing as the prayer suggests. Be still and listen for guidance.

HEAVENLY FATHER

I am asking for healing.

My body is aching, it is physical pain.

Help me to help myself.

Guide me as to what I need to do.

Be it physical, emotional, mental or spiritual.

I cannot do it alone and I know I am not alone.

May I be open and fully receptive to your grace, love and guiding light.

From there and there alone can healing come.

'Lord, thou art in me: I am in Three.'

Bless me and may I never lose sight of your unfailing love and peace.

Thank you. Amen.

A Prayer for Acceptance.

At times it can be difficult to accept situations that come our way. So when you pray for acceptance, take a few minutes to feel stillness and quietness in your heart. Breathe evenly and calmly and let your whole being settle into this stillness and quietness. Often under circumstances when acceptance is required, it is in the heart we may feel heaviness, sadness, frustration, anger, loneliness or fear. Allow your spirits to arise beyond the restless thoughts and frustrations or other emotions you may be feeling. Pray with the knowledge that fundamentally all is well and that you are loved and protected.

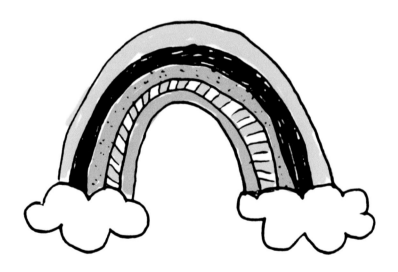

HEAVENLY FATHER

I don't have to change anything. Everything is as it should be.

I know you are there to love me and to give me strength.

Let me not be the judge, but put my faith in you. To know
this and to accept this is what will set me free.

There need never be disappointment because my faith
is strong and that faith makes me strong.

I ask for your precious words of wisdom to guide me and to help me to accept what is.

There is much to understand.

May I realise your unfailing love and be ever receptive to your guiding light.

Thank you, Amen.

It is very important to acknowledge and give thanks at the times when feeling the love of God and the joy of God in your heart. Feeling that joy within will help it to grow. It is easy to forget to pray when everything is going well in our lives. But these are the times when it is especially good to be aware of keeping that flame of love and light burning within.

Divine Mother

I come to you now with peace and love in my heart.

Feeling stillness, such inner stillness, even if only for
brief moments, I know that you are there.

If I was to ask 'Who are you? What are you?' The answer would be none
other than this sublime peace, warmth and love that I feel within.

It need never go away for I know you are Omnipresent.

I hold You in my heart.

Thank you. Amen.

A Prayer for the Stillness of God to arise within

It is so important to know and feel that Gods stillness and Peace is offered to us at all times. We are only to be receptive. This can take time and patience for us to actually allow the love of God into our lives. It helps to feel the feeling of relaxation in our body, so that the breath can flow evenly and freely. Evenness of breath, evenness of mind. Pray with sincerity and trust.

HEAVENLY FATHER

My body is still

My heart is quiet

There is stillness around me.

I now wait for your divine stillness and peace to arise within me.

I know you are there with every breath I take.

I breathe very calmly, very slowly and I feel the stillness present in every pause.

May I meet that stillness and be inside that stillness - that is, what is.

In stillness I am with You, You are with me.

Thank you. Amen

A Prayer for Joy and Love in my Life

When feeling stillness and peace in meditation, say this prayer to invoke the presence of God's love, peace and wisdom. Contemplate the deep meaning of the words that you pray. You are asking to be reminded daily of the love that is available to us. Feeling that unfailing love, we are thus able to radiate it out into the world.

HEAVENLY FATHER

Ignite the joy in my heart with your peaceful presence of love, wisdom and Divine Grace.

Remind me daily of your light and unfailing love that you radiate into the world.

I pray that I and all sentient beings be receptive to Your Love, Peace and Joy.

Thank you. Amen

PRAYER OF THANKS FOR THIS DAY.

When gratitude and joy fills your heart, say this prayer with a feeling of abundance and thanksgiving for all that is.

DIVINE MOTHER

Today I am feeling so thankful.

The blessings that come to me are visible every way I turn.

Seeing you in everything and everyone makes this happen.

Gratitude and joy fill my heart.

Please bless me always.

May I be ever receptive to your guiding light and feel your precious love all around me and within me.

Thank you. Amen

WALKING THE LABYRINTH WITH PRAYER AND MEDITATION

For quite some time now I have been visiting a Labyrinth for prayer and meditation. My personal experience has been one of curiosity, discovery, peace, calmness and inspiration. It has also been a way of opening up to numerous conversations with God.

I really relate to the Labyrinth as being a metaphor for life. As I walk I always feel comforted by the pathways within the Labyrinth resembling the twists and turns of life. And there is always the knowing that there are no dead ends and that the path leads me to the centre, a place of rest, and then returns to the threshold. Often with a renewed sense of clarity and peace.

The Labyrinth is a spiritual tool. It is a path on which to pray or it provides a space for walking meditation. In the quietness and focus on your own steps along the path, you can allow stress to dissolve. As you progress further into the walk the mind quietens and the heart opens to the energy and vibration of this sacred space.

There is really no prescriptive way to walk the Labyrinth, only to relax and to be receptive. You can bring a question to your walk or you may find a question arises during your walk. Answers do come forth, not necessarily straight away. Have faith and be patient. I often walk purely with an attitude of acceptance and gratitude which brings with it a feeling of peace and joy.

When walking, it is helpful to realize the three stages:-

- The first stage from the threshold to the centre, walk with an attitude of **'releasing'**. This can be challenging at first, so don't try to be specific, be present with each step and simply relax and breathe.
- The second stage when having arrived in the centre, allow the heart and mind to open and **'receive'**. Be still, breathe and again remember to relax. Take some time in the centre, perhaps with prayer, or be in touch with that still quiet voice within. Be still and open to all there may be to receive, without expectation. Take some time to feel your whole body relax. Connect with *your* centre and the presence of *your* God.
- The third stage is **'returning'** when walking out from the centre to the threshold. This is a wonderful opportunity to feel yourself walking in the presence of God, or your higher self, that intelligence within you that guides you towards your highest good. You are returning on this stage of the walk, with confidence, a new found clarity and a loving heart.

Labyrinths have been in existence for over 4,000 years and are found in almost every religious tradition. And more often these days in parks, hospital grounds, on private properties, retreat centres and churches. I trust that if this way of prayer and meditation appeals to you, you will find a Labyrinth, as I have, that you love to visit.

The following Prayers have come from my experiences of walking the Labyrinth.

Prayers And Meditation
At The Labyrinth

WALK THE LABYRINTH WITH AN OPEN
HEART AND MIND AND AN ATTITUDE
OF REVERENCE FOR ALL SENTIENT BEINGS

I cannot get lost if I stay on the path.

The Labyrinth shows me the way.

It gives me great joy and peace to hear those words within.

I walk for those who do not or cannot walk.

May clarity, peace and love go out to all.

May I realize that all that I need is already within.

There is nothing to attain.

God bless us all.

WHILE WALKING THE LABYRINTH

I am brimming with gratitude and joy to walk this sacred Labyrinth.

As I step onto this sacred path, I allow my heart and mind to be wide open and receptive.

I am in the moment allowing my steps to be light.

I can breathe and relax.

I can hold a question in my heart, and be open to all possibilities.

A MEDITATION AND PRAYER IN STILLNESS AFTER WALKING THE LABYRINTH

HEAVENLY FATHER

Your divine love can heal and renew our sense of Self. Our pure divine nature.

You do not wish us to be sick or negative or caught up in delusion.

You are there patiently waiting for us to wake up.

We can receive your divine love and healing whenever we allow ourselves to be receptive.

So now I pray that your Divine Grace be with me and
all those who need your healing light.

May we all be receptive and allow your healing love to manifest in our lives.

May all those who suffer feel the presence of your love and surrender to that love.

May we rest forever in your unfailing love and care.

Thank you. Amen.

A Meditation at the Labyrinth - What are my hearts desires?

With closed eyes and an open heart, I ask the question – What are my hearts desires?

I must listen in the silence of my heart.

Be calm. Do I really need to have 'hearts desires'?

When I am in the silence of my heart I have no other desire.

Everything is there.

It's like coming a full circle, not unlike the Labyrinth.

At the end, on returning, I know that all is well.

There is nothing to attain.

So I feel the peace and rest within my quiet heart.

Thank you. Amen.

Printed in the United States
By Bookmasters